Spotify Basics for Record Labels

Other Record Labels

otherrecordlabels.com

First Edition, 2022
ORLB07.2

Published by Other Record Labels.

ISBN 9798812400705
Canada

www.otherrecordlabels.com

Get the Bonus Content

This book tells the story of the basics of Spotify and how it relates to independent record labels and independent artists. It is my hope that it provides more than enough to get you on your way. However, I want to make sure that all of the tools and resources I mention in this book are relevant and up to date.

Visit **otherrecordlabels.com/spotify-bonus** for extra resources!

Be sure to join our private community of record labels at **http://facebook.otherrecordlabels.com**

And feel free to email me if you ever have any questions!

scott@otherrecordlabels.com

Table of Contents

Introduction

Streaming music has become ubiquitous. I would never assume that music tech is done evolving, but for now, it seems like streaming is here to stay.

However, with it has come many problematic components. The disappointingly low royalties make it incredibly challenging for artists to support themselves. Is "renting" music to listeners the most profitable model for artists? Are digital downloads still viable? Should fans pay more for their monthly Spotify membership? In these early years of streaming music, independent artists and record labels are blindly navigating this unfamiliar territory.

At the same time, we now know that people are paying for music more than ever before. In 2014, the average person spent approximately $55 per year on music. Today, that number is closer to $165 per year, according to Neilson. By 2020, listeners spent an average of 32 hours per week listening to music. Additionally, artists and labels of any size can reach listeners from all over the world. The barriers for entry are steadily being removed, while traditional gatekeepers have less and less control.

While recording and distribution has become more accessible and affordable, a challenging byproduct is that there has become more competition amongst artists vying to reach listeners. There are rumors that Spotify intakes nearly 100,000 new songs every day. Even if that number is an exaggeration, it still implies a seemingly insurmountable challenge to artists who want their music heard.

The solution is strategy. Record labels and independent artists need to be more intentional and strategic with how they release their music. Relying on hope that the "cream will rise to the top" is a fool's errand, and hardly ever works. The reality is that fans need to be engaged, pursued, and respected.

In this book, we will discuss a handful of simple things you can do to increase your chances of getting your music heard, getting a song placed on a playlist, and turning your streaming success into a significant revenue stream for your record label.

If I've done my job right, you will have gained a solid overview of how Spotify and the world of streaming works, the basic terminology, who the key players are, and what strategies are most effective.

CHAPTER ONE

SPOTIFY FOR ARTISTS

The first step in a record label's (or artist's) Spotify streaming strategy should be to gain access to their Spotify for Artists account. This official Spotify platform provides artists and labels with insights into their catalog's streaming numbers. The analytics provided include geographic and demographic data on their listeners, daily streaming numbers, and didactic playlist data. Let's investigate how we can gain access to these vital stats, and how we can utilize this information to help us reach more listeners.

Accessing your Spotify For Artists account.

The two easiest ways to gain access to your Spotify for Artists account is either through your digital distributor (CD Baby, TuneCore, etc.) or directly through Spotify. With the first option, your distributor can grant you access much quicker as the authorization process happens through them. Whereas, claiming your Spotify for Artists account through Spotify will require a short application and authentication process that may take a few days to have approved. (https://artists.spotify.com/claim)

Keep in mind, at the time of writing, you are not able to gain access to your Spotify for Artists account until after the artist has released at least one piece of music (single, EP, etc.).

Analyzing analytics.

Once inside your Spotify for Artists profile, you'll notice that Spotify offers an incredible number of insights into who your listeners are, and what they're listening to.

Utilize your analytics to look for what cities and

countries your artists are most popular in, which third-party playlists garner the most plays, and how your singles are performing daily.

Pitching a song to Spotify.

One of the best tools that Spotify for Artists offers is the ability to submit your upcoming single directly to their editorial team. This service provides you with a chance (albeit small) to have your song selected for a major official Spotify playlist.

Placement isn't guaranteed and can be hard to come by, but it is still worth it to take a few minutes to submit your song for consideration.

Action Step

You may be able to get access to your Spotify for Artists account right away, or it may take a few weeks to get inside. For this reason, setting up your Spotify for Artists account should be your top priority, long before you schedule your new release date. Once inside, look around and take advantage of some of the instruction videos they have for you. We will be using this tool a lot, so it is worth the time to get to know how it all works!

CHAPTER TWO

CHOOSING A DIGITAL DISTRIBUTOR

To get your music listed with the digital service providers (Spotify, Tidal, AmazonMusic, AppleMusic, etc.), you will need to choose a digital distributor (sometimes known as an "aggregator"). Digital distributors are essential and there are plenty to choose from. All of them vary in pricing and features. What follows are some things you should look out for when choosing a digital distributor.

Features of a distributor.

A few of the key features that a good digital distributor should have are, things that allow you to customize your releases. For example, make sure you can pick your own release date, add your label's name in the copyright field, as well as the ability to upload music from unlimited artists.

These are generally the features that differ amongst the platforms. Some aggregators may be cheaper and seem more appealing but withhold access to key features that make it possible for you to run your label.

Some of the most important features you will need from your digital distributor include customizing the release date, obtaining free ISRCs, free or inexpensive barcodes, distribution to the main DSPs, and instant access to your artists' Spotify for Artists accounts.

Remember, the digital distribution needs of a record label are different from the needs of an indie artist. Ensure that whichever aggregator you choose offers premium and professional features to help ensure your release is successful.

Distributor's fee structure.

Essentially, there are two different types of fee structures when it comes to aggregators. The first is an aggregator who charges a one-time fee to upload your music to all the streaming platforms. Your release remains alive in perpetuity, or until you remove it yourself. There are no annual or monthly fees that put your release in danger of expiring. An example of this type of aggregator would be CD Baby. However, there's a catch! Generally, aggregators who offer one-time distribution fees will take a small percentage of your gross streaming and download revenue. For example, CD Baby takes (approximately) 9%.

The second option would be aggregators who charge an annual fee but allow you to release as many albums and singles as you wish (depending on which annual plan you pay for). In most cases, these distributors offer various tiers that include or exclude various features. DistroKid is one of the most popular platforms that offer this structure. Another more recent platform is 3ToneMusic.com who charges $25 per year for unlimited releases, while you retain 100% of your royalties.

You'll have to choose which is right for you and your label.

Examples of distributors.

Some of the most common digital distributors (also referred to in this chapter as aggregators) include CD Baby, Amuse, ONErpm, 3tone Music, DistroKid, The Orchard, TuneCore, SOUNDROP, LANDR, and the

---

Action Step

Feel free to enter the wormhole of music blogs and YouTubers that will breakdown the pros and cons of each digital distributor. Hopefully you gain clarity and are confident in the distributor you choose. The most important thing is that you pick one and get started uploading your releases. Don't let this process overwhelm and delay your progress!

CHAPTER THREE

SPOTIFY BEST PRACTICES

A lot of artists and indie record labels overlook the impact of small things you can do when it comes to managing your Spotify profile. Spotify is a billion-dollar company, every feature they introduce has been thought-out and serves a specific purpose. Be sure to implement some of these simple things to give your artists and upcoming singles the best chance at being featured. At the very least, consider it a sacrifice to the algorithm gods...

Artist bio and photos.

Spotify for Artists offers bands and artists a chance to upload a banner photo and thumbnail photo. Be sure to upload a handful of high-resolution photos and keep them up to date. In fact, it is a good idea to refresh your press photo for every new release (single, EP, album).

In the same way, add a small artist biography to your page to build a deeper connection with your listeners. In this same section you can add a website and social media links for fans to connect with your artists in more ways.

Keeping your account up to date.

As I mentioned, when you release a new single, update your artists' press photos and bio. This shows your listeners (and Spotify) that your artists are relevant, active, and engaged.

Utilizing new features.

Periodically, Spotify (and other streaming platforms) release new apps, features, and tools for artists. For example, sometime in 2020 Spotify released Spotify Canvas; a 3-8 second video loop shown on the mobile Spotify app while a song plays. They lie somewhere between album artwork and music videos, with examples ranging from a continuous loop of animation to simple repeating video clips.

Platforms will favor users who utilize and implement their newest features, so be sure to experiment and stay up to date with any new tools Spotify releases to artists.

Action Step

Go through your Spotify for Artists profile and ensure that you've filled in every available field. The more information you provide your audience, the more touch points you create for them, the easier for them it becomes to fall in love with your music!

CHAPTER FOUR

THE TYPES OF PLAYLISTS

Not all playlists are made equal. Understanding the unique differences between official editorial playlists, third-party curators, and user-generated playlists will help you build a more effective playlist pitching strategy.

Editorial playlists.

The most popular playlists are editorial play-lists as they are official playlists created by the staff at the major digital service providers. In some cases (especially on Spotify), these playlists can have hundreds of thousand listeners that can translate into a sizable income for the artist and their record label. For this reason, they are the most evasive and hardest to get your song placed on.

Third-party playlists.

A lot of popular brands will create playlists to represent their company on Spotify and to project their brand's aesthetic. Examples of these include Starbucks, Aritzia, H&M, Sonos, etc.

Additionally, a lot of music blogs like NPR, Pitchfork, UPROXX, Digster, also have their own ongoing playlists.

User Generated Playlists (UGPs).

Don't underestimate the impact that smaller, personal playlists can have on the success of your streaming campaign. User-Generated Playlists (UGPs) are public playlists created by individual users. What makes these unique from third-party playlists is that they are often created as passion projects or as personal expressions of musical tastes.

These can be created by everyday Spotify users, social media influencers, your friends, or other independent artists.

Action Step

Make a chart in Google Sheets (or Microsoft Excel) with three columns for each of these three types of playlists. Then, list playlists you are familiar with that would be a good fit for your upcoming single release. It might even be a good idea to do this for each new single by all your artists, as songs differ greatly from one another, and may appeal to different curators and playlisters.

CHAPTER FIVE

THE ANATOMY OF A RELEASE

Digital distributors (also known as aggregators) make the upload process straightforward. Their ingestion process simplifies what would normally take hours and hours if a record label had to upload to each of the DSPs themselves. Let's break down some of the basic things you'll need when uploading your catalog to the streaming platforms.

ISRCs and barcodes.

There are two essential types of codes that will need to be associated with your new release(s). The first is a barcode, a unique barcode (not unlike the ones you scan in a grocery store) is a 12-digit UPC (Universal Product Code) that will forever be attached to your release. Singles, EPs, and albums all require their own unique barcode. In some cases, your digital distributor will provide one for free or for a nominal fee when you register your new release.

The second type of code you need to be familiar with are ISRCs, which stand for International Standard Recording Code. These are also 12-digit codes made up of numbers and letters. These codes are given to each individual song that is uploaded to the digital service providers. ISRCs are also provided by your digital distributor (free or with a small fee) and can also be provided by a mastering engineer. Some record labels will opt to purchase barcodes and ISRCs in bulk and assign them to each new release internally.

Here's an example to help you understand how barcodes and ISRCs interact with a new release: If your band releases a new 10-song album, the album itself will need a barcode, and each of the 10 songs will need their own ISRC.

However, if your band releases one of the album's songs as a pre-release single, the single will need its own barcode (different from the album) but the song will retain the same ISRC that is used when the song appears on the full-length record.

Songwriter information and genres.

Be sure to collect all the songwriter and publishing details of your artist's compositions before you prepare to upload the song(s) to your digital distributor. You will need to know exactly how many songwriters need to be included for each song.

Additionally, it is good to have the artist speak into what genre and sub-genre they consider their music to fall under. However, some streaming platforms (e.g., AppleMusic) will use their own system to determine the genre of your release, regardless of what you select.

Album artwork.

When preparing your new release for digital distribution, you will need a high-resolution JPG of your album artwork in RGB format. The bigger the better! I would suggest you ask your graphic designer to provide you with three sizes: small (500 x 500 pixels), medium (1000 x 1000 pixels), and large (3000 x 3000 pixels).

Be aware, some platforms require you to have unique artwork for each pre-release single. This means you can't use the artwork from the parent album. This varies across the board and is often inconsistent with how they treat releases from major labels. Just be aware that this may be an issue you encounter, depending on your aggregator.

Action Step

Download a free copy of my release details spreadsheet to help you organize all of the most important details of your release. Keeping the song and album details in a centralized location will make things easier for you and your artists moving forward!

Visit otherrecordlabels.com/spotify-bonus to download!

CHAPTER SIX

THE POWER OF LEAD TIME

The strategic use of lead time is key to the success of a new release. Lead time is the amount of time from the start of an album to its release date. More specifically, in marketing for a new release, I consider lead time to be the time between when the masters are complete, and when the album (or single) is released to the public.

A lot of independent artists finish recording on a Saturday, master on a Sunday, and release on a Monday. There is something beautiful about the spontaneity of home-recording, and the ease of distribution that today's technology provides. However, a negative byproduct of this immediacy is the failure of artists to give their audience the joy of anticipation. Your digital distributor will require anywhere from a few days to a few weeks to properly send your upcoming release to all the DSPs. Additionally, Spotify for Artists requires a few weeks lead time when submitting a single for editorial consideration.

Create a workback schedule.

A workback schedule is a simple to-do list that starts with the task furthest from release date leading up to tasks that are closer to the release. Like a domino, each future task requires the previous task to be completed in order to proceed. This is how a workback schedule helps you achieve a successful album release. Once you've picked a release date for your album or single, begin by working backward from that date. Identify ahead of time, any deliverables that need to be acquired for your release day to be a success.

Get ready early.

The recording phase is a great time to have conversations with the artists about their goals for this release, their tour plans, and what ideas they have for album art. It is never too early to begin planning for your release. There will always be obstacles and delays in the production or manufacturing process, having a head start provides you a margin of time for the unexpected.

Disregarding lead time.

Having sufficient lead time is something I recommended most of the time. However, there is something special about a surprise album release. Artists of all sizes and popularity levels still surprise-drop records by announcing the album's existence the day of or the day before its release. This technique uses the element of surprise as the main source of promotion. If a traditional album campaign is a jet taking off from taxiing, then a surprise album release is a rocket leaving the earth in a few seconds. But be warned, once an album (and all its potential singles) has been released out into the world, its mystery can't be reclaimed. Make sure you think twice about a surprise release, consider giving one or two singles their own day in the sun.

Action Step

Download my free Release Roadmap that will help you track your new release from the recording process right up until the official release day: Visit: otherrecordlabels. com/roadmap

CHAPTER SEVEN

PRE-RELEASE SINGLES

One release strategy that is a holdover from the 80s, 90s, and 00s is the act of releasing "singles" in the lead-up to a new album release. This strategy helps elongate your full album campaign by "teasing" select tracks from the record. While pre-release singles are by no means mandatory, it is still an incredibly effective way to build momentum for your upcoming release, while giving more album tracks their own special moment in the spotlight.

Choose 2-4 pre-release singles.

Releasing pre-release singles is something that, while you are certainly not required to do, can help lengthen your overall marketing campaign for a new release. The slow drip of new singles can help build anticipation for your upcoming full release. Furthermore, each new single campaign becomes a unique opportunity for your artist and label to reach new listeners.

You can choose anywhere between 1 - 5 songs to release prior to the album or EP release date to use as your pre-release singles. Stagger their release leading up to the album release date. For example, if your full album was set to be released on September 1st, you would want to release a first single in July, a second in early August, and a third single in late August, closer to release date.

Single mini campaigns.

Ensure that you create a mini promotion campaign around each single. This means you treat each single release as if it is a dress rehearsal for the full album release. Make a big deal about each new single, film a video or in-studio performance to share on YouTube and on social media. You can also run contests and give away 7" lathe cuts of the new song or plan an aggressive streaming campaign to try to get your new single on as many playlists as possible.

To effectively elongate your album's release campaign, it is important that you create fun and strategic mini campaigns for each pre-release single.

Singles as content.

I don't like to refer to singles or merchandise as "content" because it devalues the hard work and creativity of the artists. However, for the purpose of this chapter, it helps to think of our promotional assets as content.

Promotional assets include pre-release singles, tour dates, album title, artwork, new press photos, and other unreleased material that can help build anticipation for your new release.

Be strategic and intentional with how you release these pieces. After you've taken inventory, schedule a "slow drip" of exciting content and ensure you've picked the right platform to deliver this content to your fans.

Action Step

Look at a recent album campaign by an artist that you admire. Make a note of the album's official release date, and then look into when they released pre-release singles, and how many singles they released from the album. There is a lot we can learn from other record label's album release campaigns.

CHAPTER EIGHT

PITCHING TO PLAYLISTS

Unfortunately for talented artists, the cream doesn't always rise to the top. It would be nice if music was a meritocracy, where Spotify automatically chooses the best songs for the best playlists. But this just isn't always the case, and so we must be proactive in making sure our new singles are heard by the people (and computers) who curate playlists.

Spotify for Artists.

Utilizing the Spotify for Artists pitching tool is essential when releasing a new single. To pitch to the Spotify editorial team, you will need to have an upcoming song in queue. An upcoming single will appear in your Spotify for Artists page a few days after it has been uploaded and approved by your digital distributor.

Go through the steps and answer all the questions as it pertains to your new single. Be honest and clear about what your track sounds like, what instruments were used, and what mood the song evokes. These small details will help the editorial team (or computer algorithm) determine which Spotify playlists are ideal for your song.

It has been suggested that over a hundred thousand songs are uploaded to Spotify every day. So, temper your expectations, most songs pitched don't get placed on an official Spotify playlist. Regardless, use this free tool to pitch every upcoming single at least 3-4 weeks prior to release day to increase your chances of landing a coveted placement on an official Spotify playlist.

Third-Party, UGPs.

Third-party playlists created by brands, music curators, or social media influencers can be some of the most impactful playlists you can get your tracks on. This is because they are often human-curated, and very specific to the genre or mood they are promoting. Furthermore, the clout and brand recognition these companies or influencers bring to their playlist can help it reach a wider audience.

Start by contacting the influencers manually by locating their details on social media or on LinkedIn. A lot of reputable third-party playlists (Alex-Rainbird, IndieMono) have official submission portals on their web page. Use these submission fields and respect the process in which these curators wish to receive music.

Finally, you can reach some of these playlist curators by using a pitching platform like SubmitHub. com. SubmitHub charges a fee (that is split with the platform and submission recipient) that allows you to share your new single with very specific playlists. Not only that, but you can also filter and target user-generated playlists by genre, responsiveness, submission cost, and by their total number of followers.

Personal playlists.

Pitching your new releases to personal playlists of friends, family, and fellow artists can be as easy as simply asking them. On release day, send a DM or mass email to your closest friends, colleagues, and family members asking if they will kindly add your new single to their personal playlists. Not only will this generate a modest number of streams, it will also help improve your standing with the Spotify algorithm when they see active users saving and engaging with your new single.

Action Step

Check out the chart below to understand the various types of playlists and the ideal method for how to pitch your songs. Add a new column to the right of this chart and outline your own personal strategy for how you plan to pitch your latest single to these specific playlists.

Playlist Type	Description	How to Pitch
Editorial	Official Playlists	Spotify for Artists
Third Party	Branded Playlists	SubmitHub/Email
UGPs	Fans/Influencers	Email/Social
Discover Weekly	Algo-Created	Algorithm
Radio	Algo-Created	Algorithm
Friends/Family	Friends/Family	Personal Requests
Incidental Playlists	Unexpected Placements	Word of Mouth
Artist/Label Playlists	Your own playlists	Self-curated

CHAPTER NINE

MARKETING AND PROMOTING YOUR RELEASES

There are a few simple things you can do that will help your new releases get heard by more people. Don't rely on "hope marketing"; instead come up with an intentional strategy that gives your new songs a fighting chance.

Passive fans vs. Active fans.

Playlists provide a unique connection to passive music listeners. Active fans buy physical records, attend shows, and follow our artists on social media. Whereas passive fans may not even know who they're listening to, but they still contribute to your label's success. A record label wants and needs passive fans just as much as active fans.

Sometimes it's helpful to think of your label's streaming strategy as a funnel. At the top of your funnel (the widest part) is the passive listeners you garner from playlists.

As the funnel narrows, the audience gets smaller, but the connection strengthens. The narrowest point of your funnel will contain the smallest audience, but they'll be the most highly engaged and supportive fans.

Using this visual, we can see how playlisting plays a pivotal role in bringing new listeners into your fan funnel in a frictionless, automated way.

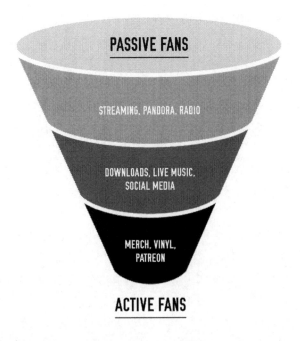

PASSIVE FANS

STREAMING, PANDORA, RADIO

DOWNLOADS, LIVE MUSIC, SOCIAL MEDIA

MERCH, VINYL, PATREON

ACTIVE FANS

Multiple actions leads to success.

Marketing thrives on compounding efforts. A well-run release campaign is often the result of 4 or 5 things (or more) going well! Implementing multiple strategies at once can increase your chances of having a successful release campaign. It is important that you aim to narrow your focus down to smaller, manageable tasks and ideas that contribute to the overall success of your record label.

To rely solely on a Pitchfork review is foolish. Putting all your chips on the hopes of getting a song placed on a prominent HBO show is irresponsible. These are all great ambitions to have, but they must be paired with multiple strategies that vary in achievability. Diversify your chances of success by pursuing as many promotional opportunities available to you. Some of the things may seem small and insignificant on their own, but when used in combination they can produce enormous results.

Make it easy for fans.

You'd be surprised at how often independent artists become their own greatest obstacle. It should go without saying that your fans should be able to stream and hear your music as quickly and painlessly as possible. Provide pre-save links to your audience that is compatible with their streaming platform of choice (AppleMusic, Spotify, Tidal, etc.).

Additionally, you can embed a Spotify player into your website that plays your latest release or a compilation playlist that you've made to promote your label's tracks.

Take an audit of your web presence – or have a friend or family member do it, with you watching over their shoulder –and see how easy it would be for a new visitor to quickly sample your music.

Action Step

Create a Spotify playlist that includes some of your record label's best tracks. Anywhere between 10 and 40 songs is a good number to aim for. Once you've created this playlist, embed it on your website, add it to your link-in-bio menu, and DM it to your artists to share on their platforms. You could even blitz your friends and family and ask them to add the playlist to their library, just to bolster the follower number!

CHAPTER TEN

MANAGING ROYALTIES FROM STREAMING

Earning a million plays means nothing if you don't know how to get paid from those streams! It is also vitally important that record labels know how to accurately calculate the royalties that are owed to their artists based on the data from digital distributors.

Net payments from your distributor.

Revenue from the streaming platforms gets paid directly to your aggregators (CD Baby, 3Tone Music, DistroKid, Amuse, etc.). Your aggregator then pays you monthly or once your revenue reaches a specific threshold. Keep in mind, these royalties can be many months behind. For example, you may receive a payment in April for streams that occurred in January.

Payments generally come in a lump sum that includes all streaming revenue from your entire catalog (all artists and releases). A good aggregator should also provide you with a detailed spreadsheet that includes a breakdown of streams that you can sort by artist and/or release.

Using this spreadsheet, you should be able to easily tally the total net amount (revenue minus aggregator fees, PayPal fees, etc.) that the artist generated in a certain period of time.

Aggregator splits vs. Label accounting.

There are two common ways you can manage

and collect the revenues that you generate from the streaming platforms.

Some digital distributors like DistroKid provide a tool that will automatically split a certain percentage of your streaming revenue and pay your artists directly. Unfortunately, artists need to be a paying DistroKid subscriber to receive a payment.

You may find this splitting tool to be a convenient feature for your record label. However, it fails to consider any expenses you as the record label may have incurred when promoting the release. Depending on the terms of your agreement with the artist, you may be entitled to deduct some (or all) of these expenses before paying the artist a royalty.

The alternative is for you as a record label to collect all the net revenue from digital sales (post payment processing fees), and then distribute the appropriate amount to your artists individually. Using a record label accounting tool like Infinite Catalog (otherrecordlabels.com/directory) can help make this process run smoothly.

Common royalty splits.

While there are common royalty splits that we see often, there is no hard and fast rule when it comes to splitting digital royalties with your artists. The most common split when it comes to digital, sync, and physical royalties is 50/50. That means 50% of net profits goes to the artist and 50% goes to the record label. For larger indie labels and major labels, the percentage for the artist significantly decreases, based on the influence and size of the record label.

Here is where things can get unique to your own record label: if you are a label that has a lot of experience in the streaming universe and has a proven track record when it comes to playlisting, then taking a higher percentage of streaming royalties may be justified (e.g., 65% for the label, 35% for the artist). Conversely, if your record label specializes in vinyl or cassette sales and lacks the capacity and know-how to create a successful streaming campaign, perhaps it may make sense to take a much smaller percentage of the revenue from streaming (e.g., 10% for the label, 90% for the artist).

Action Step

Learn more about managing your record label royalties by checking our royalty resources (including an incredibly powerful software service from our friends at Infinite Catalog).
Visit otherrecordlabels.com/royalties

Conclusion

Throughout the pages in this book, there are macro strategies that you may implement over the course of the next several months, as you release new music. At the same time, there are smaller, micro concepts that you can implement today to help your artists reach new listeners on Spotify. It is important to note that success in music comes not from any singular action, but from the compounding of many small actions.

Don't underestimate this compounding power of small improvements. You may feel miles away from reaching the goals you've set out for your record label, but you won't get there with one giant leap. Instead, take multiple, small steps forward. Streaming revenue should make up just one piece of the pie, while other diverse sources of revenue form the other slices. Your goal of having a sustainable record label that supports the livelihood of creatives is possible if you view these strategies as incremental improvements. On their own, they may not make a noticeable impact, but together they can amount to something great.

I hope this small book has helped demystify Spotify and the world of music streaming for you. However, there is so much more for us to learn in this space. Attend conferences, network with other record labels and musicians. Be helpful, humble, and passionate in your record label journey. Most importantly, don't forget to celebrate your streaming milestones, no matter if the number is a million streams or one hundred; be proud of your growth, and keep growing!

Additional Resources

Trusted Vendors, Attorneys, Service Providers
Visit our Directory to access a short list of hand-picked industry vendors that can help you and your artists with things like bio writing, royalty accounting, music law, and radio promotions.
otherrecordlabels.com/directory

Book Recommendations
I constantly maintain a list of music industry and business books that I think will help you in your record label journey.
otherrecordlabels.com/books

Record Label Toolkit
Get access to sample recording contracts, marketing checklist, release roadmap, and a free record label business plan.
otherrecordlabels.com/toolkit

Record Label Facebook Community

Join our private Facebook group for independent record label employees and owners.

facebook.otherrecordlabels.com

Be Your Own Record Label

A resource for independent artists who self-manage their own career to discover what they can learn from record labels.

otherrecordlabels.com/toolbox

Streaming Resources

Stay up-to-date with all of our resources and recommendations on the topic of streaming and playlists!

otherrecordlabels.com/streaming

Spotify Basics FAQs

Here is a list of some of the common Spotify, play-lists, and streaming questions I hear from folks in our record label community. Some of these questions have been answered in the pages above, but I thought it would be helpful to consolidate them together in one place.

How do I get my music on Spotify playlists?

At the time of writing this, the only way to get on an official Spotify playlist is to use the Spotify for Artists portal to pitch your new singles. This should be done 2-6 weeks prior to release day, and you should have a well thought out pitch and artist bio prepared for when you are submitting a new song.

Having said that, some artists do appear on official Spotify playlists from time to time, without using the Spotify for Artists submission tool.

In addition to official Spotify editorial playlists, there are also third-party playlists that are often just as impactful as official playlists. To get on one of these playlists, you must find out how they accept submissions. In some cases, you can email the curators directly (or DM them on social media). Some third-party playlists have their own submission portals on their website (IndieMono, AlexRainbirdMusic) and some playlists utilize tools like SubmitHub to manage their submissions.

How do I transfer an album that an artist self-released, to my record label's account?

There are generally two ways to go about doing this. If you and your artist use the same aggregators (e.g., CD Baby, DistroKid), you may be able to contact the distributor to conduct the transfer on your behalf. They will likely need explicit permission from both parties, as well as album details like title, barcode, etc.

Another option would be for the artist to remove their album from the streaming platforms by canceling their distribution contract with their aggregator. Once this process is in motion, the record label can then re-upload the songs using their own distributor. If you want, you could create new album artwork, a different track listing, or an entirely new album title. However, before the artist deletes their album, they should attempt to acquire the ISRCs for each of their songs. These codes should be used by the record label on the new release, to retain and transfer the streaming data (play count, etc.).

Can I bypass the aggregators and upload directly to Spotify myself?

At the time of writing this, no, you cannot. There was a short window of time when Spotify was piloting a project to allow artists to upload directly to Spotify. This program no longer exists. Even when it did exist, it was problematic, as it still required artists to use another distributor to upload the same songs to AppleMusic, Tidal, and all the other streaming platforms.

Using a digital aggregator ensures that your music is uploaded to every possible streaming platform worldwide, even ones you've never heard of. Regardless of how arduous and time-consuming this process would be, as of right now, independent labels and artists are not permitted to upload directly to the streaming platforms.

How much is the Spotify royalty rate?

Nobody knows for sure; it is one of the greatest mysteries of the world. Having said that, recent estimates put the number somewhere around $0.00318 per stream*. This means it would take approximately 315 plays to earn a dollar, or 31,500 to earn $100, or 31.5 million plays to earn $100,000!

*This estimate is based on a loose average and can't officially be verified. For example, I have a variety of different royalty rates in my distributor account ranging from $0.00176642 to $0.00734465 per stream.

Should I release a single, EP, or full length?

I tend to think of these three formats as a natural evolution for a new artist. It's always best to test the waters with a single, perhaps a few singles. After you've established your artist profile on DSPs – and learned what your audience enjoys – you can compile a few old songs and new songs into a new EP. Finally, a full-length record is something an artist should work towards, perhaps a year or two into their career launch.

Keep in mind that each of these three release levels require a greater amount of promotional attention. A full-length album comes with a more arduous marketing process that can include a publicist, manufacturing, multiple pre-release singles, a tour, and album merchandise.

Should I pay a service to get my music on playlists?

Absolutely not. There are black market services that will charge you $50-$100 and guarantee a bulk number of streams. You may think this is a good investment to help your artist look legitimate, but the fact is that this will throw up serious red flags with Spotify, and it may get blacklisted on their platform, or at worst, banned altogether. There are a few legitimate websites that aggregate data about playlists and their curators. Some of these websites charge a fee (Playlist Push, SubmitHub, Chartmetric) and provide contact information and listener data on a swath of official and unofficial Spotify playlists. The purpose of these tools is to find relevant and authentic playlists that you can build relationships with who you think would appreciate your releases.

Do I need to have our releases professionally mastered?

Music tech has come a long way, and you technically don't need to have your music mastered. You can upload your songs to DistroKid or CDBaby or Bandcamp whether they are mastered or not (it is reported that Spotify enacts a basic amount of volume leveling to all songs). Having said that, there's nothing quite like a professionally mastered release. A great mastering engineer takes into consideration all the various listening platforms that your audience may use. This helps the music sound best on any device and on any format. Check out some of our recommended vendors, including mastering engineers in our Directory: otherrecord-labels.com/directory.

How much does a label take from the artist?

Major labels have been known to take upwards of 90% of net sales. Mid-size independents' royalty rates average between 50-75%. The most common royalty share amongst small indie labels is 50/50. You can even offer a more lopsided royalty in favor of your artist, something like 35% for the label and 65% for the artist.

Glossary

Aggregator - This is an online paid service that distributes your music to the streaming platforms (DSPs). Examples of digital aggregators are CD Baby, 3Tone Music, Awol, DistroKid, Ditto, Tunecore.

Album Cycle - This term refers to the time period where an artist is promoting their release. This could be a few months leading up to the release and it also includes the year or so after the release where the artist is on tour.

Catalog - This would refer to all the releases (or titles) on your record label. This would include previously released singles, EPs, and albums.

DSPs - This term stands for Digital Service Providers and it refers to streaming platforms such as Spotify, Amazon Music, AppleMusic, Tidal, etc.

ISRCs - International Standard Recording Code. A code provided to each recording that is released to the digital service providers. This code is provided for free (or for a small fee) by the digital distributors and mastering engineers.

PROs - Performing Rights Organizations (e.g., PRS, ASCAP, SESAC) help songwriters and publishers get paid for the usage of their music by collecting performance royalties on their behalf.

Master Rights - The rights to the sound recording of the song. The owner of these rights (artist or record label) grants the rights of the master to be used.

Metadata - Music metadata is the collection of information that pertains to a song file, such as artist name, album title, year, record label, genre, lyrics, description, composers, and many other details about the recording. This information can be embedded into a MP3 file.

Sync - Sync is short for synchronization which refers to the act of synchronizing a song to a visual medium (movie, commercial, YouTube video).

Further Reading

All You Need to Know About the Music Business: 10th Edition by Donald S. Passman

The Plain & Simple Guide to Music Publishing by Randall D. Wixen

How to Start a Record Label: A 30 Day Guide by Scott Orr

Work Hard Playlist Hard: The DIY playlist guide for Artists and Curator by Mike Warner

The War of Art: Break Through the Blocks and Win Your Inner Creative Battles by Steven Pressfield

More recommendations found at:
otherrecordlabels.com/books

Other Record Labels Podcast
The Art and Culture of Running a Record Label

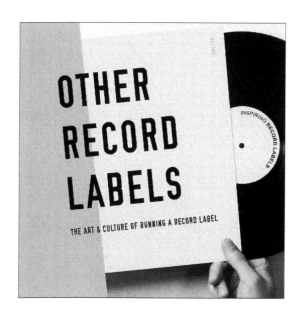

Listen to interviews and insights from today's independent record labels including Sub Pop Records, Asthmatic Kitty Records, Mute Records, Ghostly International, Z Tapes, Asian Man Records, Jagjaguar, and more!

Listen wherever you get your podcasts.

otherrecordlabels.com/listen

About the Author

Scott Orr is the host of *Other Record Labels*, a podcast about the art and culture of running a record label. Scott also runs Other Songs, a label he started in 2010. He lives and works in Ontario, Canada. He has two kids, and one of them is his favorite.

Instagram: @otherrecordlabels, @scott.orr

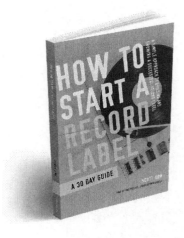

**How to Start a Record Label:
A 30 Day Guide**
Available on Amazon

**Record Label Productivity
Planner**
Available on Amazon

otherrecordlabels.com/books

SPECIAL BONUS FOR YOU!
Get 30% Off Our Online Courses

Kindly review this book on Amazon and then go to
otherrecordlabels.com/thankyou
to instantly access your 30% off coupon!

Notes

Notes

_____

_____

_____

_____

_____

_____

_____

_____

_____

_____

_____

_____

_____

_____

_____

_____

_____

_____

_____

_____

_____

Notes

Notes

otherrecordlabels.com

Printed in Great Britain
by Amazon

24124115R00051